dog training

understanding and
caring for your pet

Written by
Julia Barnes

dog training

understanding and
caring for your pet

Written by
Julia Barnes

Magnet & Steel Ltd

www.magnetsteel.com

ISBN: 978-1-907337-23-9
ISBN: 1-907337-23-7

Contents

Why train
your dog?

Why train your dog?

Owning a well-trained dog is nothing but a pleasure. You have a dog that does as he is asked, fits in with your lifestyle, and can be relied on to behave impeccably in a variety of different situations.

This is what you want – but can it be achieved? The short answer is: yes it can, but only if you are prepared to work at it. A dog does not come into your home knowing what is considered acceptable behaviour. He has no knowledge of 'good' or 'bad'; he needs to be taught how to behave.

We have a good starting point in that a dog retains the instincts of a pack animal, and is prepared to look for leadership and find his place in the human pack that he is to be part of.

You need to provide that leadership so that you have a dog that respects you, but also one that loves and trusts you. There are a number of ways in which you can build this relationship:

Spend time with your dog so that he really gets to know you and vice versa.

Make sure you are, generally, the person who feeds the dog so he sees you as the ultimate provider.

Allocate times to groom and handle your dog so he accepts you completely – even if you are carrying out tasks such as nail trimming, which are invasive.

Be consistent with your dog so he always knows what is expected of him.

Have fun with your dog; this includes going for walks, playing games and training, so your dog looks to you for mental stimulation.

If you keep your side of the bargain and establish a good relationship with your dog through consistency and training, you will be rewarded a thousand-fold.

For the family

If you are bringing a dog into your family, it is even more important that he learns to fit in with your lifestyle. You can work on having a one-on-one relationship with your dog – but what happens when you are not around?

A dog has to understand his place in the family pack – and this means that he must respect every person that he lives with. Obviously, he is not going to view everyone in exactly the same light; he will have the strongest bond with the person who feeds him, trains him, and exercises him. But he must live alongside, and in harmony with, everyone – right down to the smallest child.

A dog that does not learn his place in the family pack can be a major problem:

He will have no respect for other people's space, and will push and barge his way around, so that he is always first in line.

He will demand attention by barking and jumping up.

He will not understand how to play safely, nor the need to inhibit his instinct to bite and give up toys on request.

This type of behaviour is, at best, difficult to live with but, at worst, it is highly dangerous, particularly if you have toddlers and young children in your family.

Golden rules

If you follow the rules outlined below, alongside general training and socialisation, you will have a dog that is perfectly equipped to fit in with family life. Play with small children should always be supervised. This is particularly true if you have a puppy. It only tales a second for a game to get out of hand, with potentially dire consequences.

Teach children how to behave around a dog, stroking him gently, and not pulling his ears, or treating him like a toy.

It is natural for puppies to mouth – watch a litter of pups playing together and you will see how rough they can be with each other. If you have a puppy you need to teach him to inhibit this instinct (see Good Manners page 88), and this lesson should be continually reinforced with older dogs.

Teach your dog to give up toys on request (see Good Manners: page 88).

Children must never disturb a dog when he is eating or sleeping.

Puppies and young dogs (and some breeds in particular) are excited by movement, so games that involve running and chasing should be very carefully monitored.

Shouting and screaming should be firmly discouraged as this creates a charged atmosphere where a dog could easily become over-excited.

Children must be taught not to tease the dog with toys or with food.

If you have a puppy or a young dog, make sure children eat at the table so the pup understands food is off limits.

Teach your dog that he gets attention when all four feet are on the ground – not when he jumps up at you, or the children (see Correcting Your Dog, page 70).

For the community

Your dog is not only a part of your family, he is a member of the community, and he needs to learn how to be a good citizen. Regardless of whether you are a dog lover, or whether you are anti-dog, no one likes a dog that is a menace in public places.

Anti-social behaviour may involve the following:

- Barking or jumping up at strangers.

- Chasing livestock.

- Bullying other dogs.

- Chasing after joggers, bikes, and sometimes even passing traffic.

- Fouling public places. This is entirely your responsibility, and you must make sure that you clean up after your dog whenever you go outside your own home.

Programme of socialisation

The root cause of anti-social behaviour in dogs is lack of socialisation. This is the process of teaching your dog about the world he lives in, so that he does not feel frightened, alarmed or threatened when he encounters new situations and new experiences. Social education starts when a puppy is taught how to behave by his mother and by interacting with his littermates. The breeder will continue the process, exposing the pups to the sights and sounds of a busy household, and giving them the opportunity to meet people of all ages.

When a puppy arrives in his new home, he should undergo a comprehensive programme of socialisation throughout his first year – and beyond – so you end up with a dog that will be calm and relaxed in all situations.

There are many elements involved in socialising your dog. Try all, or some, of the following:

Invite visitors to the house and ask them to wear a hat, carry a stick, an umbrella or a backpack, so your dog gets used to people – and their appendages.

Accustom your dog to traffic, starting off in a quiet neighbourhood and progressing to a busier area as he becomes more confident.

Go to a children's play area and let your dog watch for a while. He will get used to the noise – shouts, laughter and tears – and, if you do not have children of your own, he will get the chance to meet some.

Go to an outdoor market crowded with shoppers, trolleys, and pushchairs. Your dog will learn how to walk through crowds and get used to the shouts of vendors. You can encourage him to resist the more enticing smells coming from the food stalls and the burger van.

Go to training classes. These are useful in helping you to train your dog, but they also give dogs the opportunity to meet each other in a controlled situation, and to work alongside each other.

Organise a walk in the park with a friend who has a dog of sound temperament. This will give him the opportunity to play with another dog, and perfect his canine good manners.

Go to a railway station. You don't have to actually go on a train – your dog will learn a lot just by walking along a platform. He will hear and see trains, walk up and down stairs and maybe over a bridge, as well as seeing people wheeling suitcases, and hearing loudspeaker announcements.

A country fair is a great place to socialise your dog, regardless of whether you live in the town or in the country. You will see livestock in pens – cows, sheep, goats, and poultry – there will be a variety of farm machinery, lots of stalls, possibly a bouncy castle, and there may even be a horse or a dog show in progress.

For your dog

Last – but certainly not least – you should train your dog in order to give him a better life. Do not think, for one moment, that you are being kind-hearted if you neglect his education. It is exactly the same as spoiling a child; you may be giving the child what he wants, but this is not what he needs.

A dog is a pack animal, and despite thousands of years of domestication, he still views the world from this perspective. A pack works effectively because members co-operate, under the guidance of a leader or a leading pair, to ensure their survival. A pack will hunt together, face danger together, and help to raise offspring together. Although there is a pack hierarchy, there is an overwhelming sense of co-operation and social cohesion, because this serves the interests of each individual as well as the pack as a whole.

When a dog comes into your family, he is looking for a provider – someone who gives him food, care, and shelter – but he is also looking for a social structure to be a part of. He wants to integrate with his human pack, but he also wants a decision-maker so that he feels safe and secure, and understands what is expected of him.

When you take on a dog, you must become his provider, his teacher and his leader. If a dog understands where the boundaries lie, he will have the confidence to enjoy life to the full, and establish relationships – both human and canine – that will be fulfilling and enriching.

Your job is not to bully your dog into doing what he is told, or to leave him to his own devices. You must take on the responsibility of teaching him what is, and what is not, acceptable behaviour. You will need to do this in the home, and when you go out, encouraging your dog to be calm, well behaved and relaxed. He will be happy in his role as trusted and treasured family companion – and you will be rewarded with a dog that will give you his undying love and respect.

Great
expectations

Dogs are the most versatile of all pets
– they can perform many different roles
depending on what you want from your
dog – and how much work you are
prepared to put in...

Family companion

Your dog's role as your family companion is a dog's finest role and should never be under estimated. However, a pet dog still needs to learn a variety of social skills and training exercises so that he is easy to live with, and can be kept safe from danger, but he does not have to become a specialist. The great majority of dogs are entirely content with this role, and as long as they can spend quality time with their family, they ask for nothing more.

All pedigrees – and non-pedigrees – can make outstanding pets. The only major consideration is to choose a dog that will fit in with your lifestyle.

In practical terms, this means:

Do you have a house and a car that is big enough to accommodate one of the larger breeds, such as a Great Dane or a St Bernard?

Do you have time to devote to grooming one of the glamorous longcoated breeds, such as a Yorkshire Terrier or an Afghan Hound?

Are you fit enough – and do you have sufficient time – to take on an energetic breed, such as an English Springer Spaniel or a Beagle?

Can you cope with a breed that needs extra mental stimulation and training, such as Border Collie or a German Shepherd Dog?

You also need to consider the make-up of your family. If you have small children, a Toy Dog may not be the best choice; you would be better going for a more robust breed, such as a Labrador Retriever.

Good citizens

If you want to own a well-behaved pet dog, join a training club that runs the Kennel Club's Good Citizen award scheme. This consists of a series of tests, starting with puppy foundation and progressing from bronze to silver and finally to the coveted gold award. The tests are designed to examine your dog's behaviour, focusing on basic training exercises and social skills with people and other dogs. There is also a section that evaluates your own dog knowledge and your responsibilities as an owner. The Good Citizen Scheme is not too demanding, but it is an excellent way of working with your dog and achieving a standard you can be proud of.

Obedience

Do you have ambitions to train your dog to compete in Obedience competitions? This is a demanding sport which requires precision and accuracy, so it is not for every owner – or for every dog. The tests, which include heelwork, retrieves, sendaway, recall, distant control, stays and scentwork, get progressively more difficult as you progress, with the handler giving a minimum of guidance to the dog.

In the USA, a wide variety of breeds compete in Obedience with considerable success. In the UK, the Obedience world is dominated by Border Collies, German Shepherd Dogs, Belgian Shepherds, and some of the Gundog breeds. However, there is no reason not to have a go with any breed – you never know how far you might get.

To compete in Obedience, you need a good foundation in basic training, and then you will need to find a club that specialises in Competitive Obedience. There are also instructors who will give one-on-one tuition. You can find them on the internet.

Agility

This sport has grown enormously in popularity – and it really is open to all, pedigree or non-pedigree, large or small. Dogs cannot start competing until they are 18 months of age, as negotiating the equipment could put strain on vulnerable joints while they are still growing.

The equipment includes:

- Jumps (upright and long jump)
- Tunnels (rigid and collapsible)
- Weaves
- A-frame
- Dog walk
- Seesaw
- Tyre

The course is timed, and penalties are given for knocking poles down, missing weaves, missing contact points on the A-frame, dog walk or seesaw, and refusals. If you take the wrong course, you and your dog will be eliminated. Dogs progress up the grades as they win out.

Classes are divided into small, medium and large, depending on the size of dog – so any breed from a Chihuahua to a Great Dane can compete. Border Collies excel at this sport, though Australian Kelpies are also proving highly successful at the top level. Among the small breeds, Jack Russells, Border Terriers and Cocker Spaniels from working lines do very well, but, regardless of breed, if you can get your dog really motivated, you will be surprised how fast he can go.

If you want to get involved in Agility, you will need to find a specialist club in your area.

Flyball

Flyball is a team sport; the dogs love it, and it is undoubtedly the noisiest of all the canine sports! Four dogs are selected to run in a relay race against an opposing team. The dogs are sent out by their handlers to jump four hurdles, catch the ball from the flyball box, and then return over the hurdles.

At the top level, this sport is fast and furious, and although it is dominated by Border Collies, many other breeds, such as Belgian Shepherds, English Springer Spaniels, Labradors and Jack Russells – as well as mongrels and crossbreeds – make a big contribution. This is particularly true in multi-breed competitions, where the team is made up of four dogs of different breeds, only one of which can be a Border Collie. Points are awarded to dogs and teams. Annual awards are given to top dogs and top teams, and milestone awards are given out to dogs as they attain points throughout their flyballing careers.

There are specialist Flyball clubs throughout the country if you want to have a go.

Working trials

This is a very challenging sport that was originally based on requirements needed for working police dogs. However, it has been adapted so that smaller breeds can also take part. The sport consists of three basic components:

Control

Dog and handler must complete obedience exercises, but the work does not have to be as precise as it is in Competitive Obedience.

Agility

Dogs must negotiate a hurdle, a long jump and a scale (heights vary depending on the size of the dog).

Nosework

The dog must follow a track that has been laid over a set course. The surface may vary, and the length of time between the track being laid and the dog starting work is increased in the advanced classes.

The breeds associated with Working Trials are German Shepherd Dogs, Border Collies, Belgian Shepherds, Rottweilers, Dobermanns, and some of the Gundog breeds, such as Labrador Retrievers, Golden Retrievers, German Shorthaired Pointers, and Weimaraners. However, a number of smaller breeds, such as Cocker Spaniels and Border Terriers, are also making their mark. Again, your dog does not need to be a pedigree to compete.

If you want to get involved in Working Trials, you will need to find a specialist club or a trainer that specialises in the sport.

Dancing with dogs

This is a relatively new competitive discipline for dogs, but it already has an enthusiastic following. Dancing with your dog may sound easy – but do not be deceived. Choreographing a routine to music is a major challenge, and it takes a long time, and a lot of patience to teach a dog the moves and tricks that are required to create an interesting and varied routine.

Dancing with dogs is divided into two categories: Heelwork to Music and Canine Freestyle. In Heelwork to Music, the dog must work closely with his handler and show a variety of close 'heelwork' positions. In Canine Freestyle, the routine can be more flamboyant, with the dog working at a distance from the handler and performing spectacular tricks. Routines are judged on style and presentation, content and accuracy.

Any dog – no matter how big or small – can take part. But it certainly helps if you have a dog that enjoys the challenge of learning new things. Most handlers train their own dogs for this discipline, but you can also attend workshops and get one-on-one tuition.

Showing

If you have a pedigree dog, you may decide you want to get involved in the world of showing. In this discipline, dogs are assessed against the Breed Standard, which is a written 'blueprint' describing the perfect specimen. The judge will examine each dog, evaluating conformation coat, colour, temperament and movement. It is the dog who, in the judge's opinion, adheres most closely to the Breed Standard, that will be placed first.

Showing is very competitive at the top level – and very addictive. Ideally, you should make your plans when you first buy a puppy so you invest in a dog that has show potential. You will then need to train him for the ring, and if you have a high maintenance breed, such as a Yorkshire Terrier or a Poodle, you will need to learn how to present your dog for the show ring.

There are many clubs that hold ringcraft classes, and this is a good place to start if you decide that showing is for you.

Winning ways

Pedigree dogs are placed in groups, depending on their original function. In the UK there are seven groups:

Pastoral
Working
Hounds
Toys
Terriers
Gundogs
Utility

Each breed is judged individually, and the dog that is judged Best of Breed will go forward to be judged in his group. The group winner will then compete against the other six group winners – and it is the dog that is selected as the winner of all the groups that is awarded Best in Show.

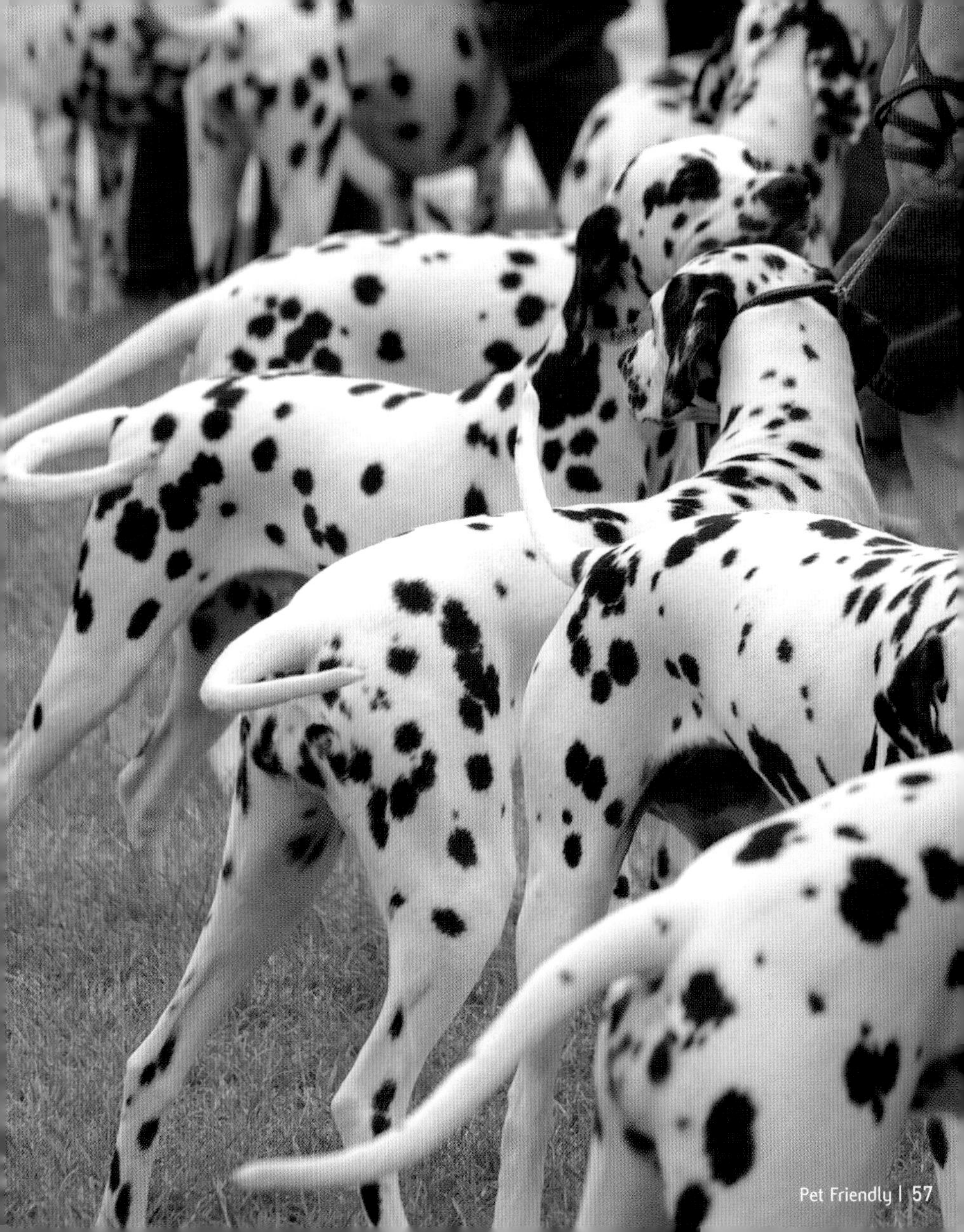

Rewarding your dog

When you see a highly-trained dog, the first question that most people ask is: "Why does he do it?

Why should a sniffer dog work tirelessly to find drugs and explosives, why should an assistance dog get the clothes out of the washing machine for his disabled owner, and why should a dog execute immaculate heelwork in an Obedience competition, never stepping a centimetre out of line?

The answer is always the same: a dog repeats behaviour because he has discovered that it is rewarding for him. The handler teaches him to expect a reward for carrying out a task – and the dog works to get his reward. The more he values the reward, the keener he will be to work for it. So, if you see a dog complete a given task – such as searching a suitcase for contraband – he will instantly get a reward. In most cases, this will be a game with a favourite toy.

This is the foundation of all positive, reward-based training, which has proved to be the most effective method of teaching dogs. It applies to all aspects of dog training – from teaching a puppy to sit, to training an assistance dog to operate an elevator switch.

Finding a reward

What does a dog perceive as the best reward he can get? Every dog is an individual so, to some extent, it is a matter of getting to know your dog and finding out what he most values. However, there are tried and trusted rewards that appeal to most dogs.

It is also important to remember that you can have more than reward; you can change your reward, or use a combination of rewards to keep training fresh and interesting.

Food

For many dogs, food is seen as the biggest reward. There are some breeds, such as the Labrador Retriever, that are the 'foodies' of the dog world and will consider a mere morsel of dry biscuit worth working for. Other dogs take a bit more tempting, and will value treats such as cheese, cooked liver or sausage.

Some trainers grade their treats and will give 'everyday treats' – dry kibble, for example – for random rewards, such as when asking a dog to sit to have his lead attached. They will save high-value treats until they are teaching something new.

If you are using food treats as rewards, make sure you deduct what you are giving from your dog's daily ration. You may think treats do not amount to much, but they can soon add up, particularly if you are using cheese or sausage, which are high in calories.

An overweight dog is lazy and lethargic and will have little interest in training. Worse still, obesity leads to many health problems and will almost certainly shorten your dog's life expectancy.

Toys

Some dogs prefer a game with a toy to any food reward. This tends to apply to breeds that naturally have a strong work ethic, such as Border Collies and German Shepherds, but the key is to make a toy exciting for your dog. It helps if you start this early on when a puppy is keen to play, and to make games interactive, so your dog is enjoying playing with you, rather than simply with a toy.

If you decide to use a toy as a reward, keep it out of the dog's reach and only use it when you are training. In this way, it has added value for your dog.

Physical praise

Dogs are tactile and they enjoy being stroked and patted. When your dog has done something correctly, a stroke can be used to praise him. Some dogs are very physical, and if they get a good rub down, they know they have done well!

Verbal praise

Verbal communication is more important to us than it is to our dogs – but it is still a useful tool. Dogs understand tone of voice, and if you use a warm, happy, encouraging tone, your dog will respond positively, knowing that you are pleased with him.

Correcting your dog

We would all like to think that are dogs are perfectly behaved and never put a paw out of place. But there are times when a dog will push his luck and cross a boundary or, more frequently, a dog may make a mistake in training that needs to be corrected.

In the old-fashioned school of dog training, it was considered perfectly acceptable to punish a dog for stepping out of line, or for getting something wrong. Harsh yanks on a choke chain were the order of the day, and dogs obeyed out of fear, rather than a desire to work and earn a reward.

Fortunately, we have come a long way in understanding dog mentality, and harsh handling is universally condemned. It is potentially harmful for the dog, and it simply does not work. You may make some progress by coercing your dog into co-operation. But it will be negligible compared with the results you get from a happy, willing pupil who works because he knows he will be rewarded.

Who is to blame?

Before you decide how to correct your dog, you must first establish the cause of the problem – and it may well be that it is something you are doing wrong. This applies regardless of whether you are trying to prevent undesirable behaviour, or whether you are struggling to teach your dog a new exercise.

Ask yourself the following questions:

Does the dog understand what you want him to do?

If your dog is confused, there is very little chance of success. If you are teaching an exercise, break it down into small steps to facilitate learning. This will also give you the chance to reward him for 'getting it right', rather than trying to correct something he does not understand.

If you are trying to stop undesirable behaviour, such as jumping up, does your dog understand what you consider inappropriate, or does he think that being pushed down is all part of a game?

Are you being clear in the way you are giving instructions?

Dogs do not speak English, even though we act as though they do. Therefore, a string of words telling your dog he is naughty, and he mustn't do it again because you will be cross with him, is pretty meaningless. It is also pointless to keep repeating the same command or shouting his name again and again – as far as your dog is concerned, you are simply babbling and he will tune out completely.

Are you being consistent, or are you muddling your dog with mixed messages?

We do have a tendency to expect our dogs to be mind-readers – of course, your dog should know he can jump up at you when you are in a soppy, playful mood, but he certainly must not jump up when you are dressed in your best clothes and ready to go out.

As far as the dog is concerned there is no difference in what he has done – but your reaction is one of two extremes. How is he meant to deal with this? The simple answer is that he cannot, and it unfair to expect him to do so. You must be 100 per cent consistent with your dog, so that he understands that the rules you have laid down always apply.

The same need for consistency applies when you are training your dog. If you are working on a new exercise, always use the same verbal cues and body language, so he knows what is expected of him.

Are you rewarding the dog for the behaviour you want, rather than the behaviour you do not want?

This may sound rather silly – of course you are not going to reward your dog for something you don't want him to do. However, you may be doing that very thing unintentionally.

For example, your dog is barking because you have shut him in the kitchen, so you shout at him to be quiet. Your dog is demanding your attention, and you have instantly rewarded him by responding. He does not mind that you shouted at him– he wanted attention and that is what you gave him. You cannot be surprised when he carries on barking because, as far as he is concerned, it got the result he wanted.

Finding a way forward

There are a number of effective methods of correcting behaviour, but these should only be applied when you have got to the root of the problem and you are able to communicate clearly with your dog.

As we have seen, dogs respond to tone of voice; this can be used negatively, as well as when we are being positive and giving praise. A firm, deep voice will tell your dog that you mean business. If you catch him red-handed, stealing from the bin, a harsh "No" which sounds like a warning growl, will be effective. You can counter this by using your warm, encouraging voice immediately afterwards, inviting him to "Come' and then rewarding him with lots of fuss.

If your dog has gone wrong in a training exercise, do not use a harsh tone of voice to correct him. You can say something like "Try again", but use a completely neutral tone – neither praising, nor reprimanding – so that he knows he must work a bit harder to get his reward.

Ignoring your dog

This training tool is vastly under-rated, because 'doing nothing' does not seem very pro-active. However, it is a message that hits home, and most dogs will quickly change their behaviour because they can see that what they are doing is not working.

For example, your dog jumps up at you, so you tell him off and push him down. As we have seen, this reaction is highly rewarding for a dog that wants attention – and so he will keep on repeating it. However, if he jumps up at you, and you turn away, avoid eye contact, and make no physical contact, he is not getting what he wants. He may jump up a couple more times to try to make you react. But if you continue to ignore him, he will stop and think of another strategy.

This is the moment, when the dog has all four feet on the ground, that you come to life. Give him lots of praise and stroke him – making sure he does not get too excited and tries to jump up again. The lesson he is learning is that when he jumps up he is ignored, and when he has all four feet on the ground, he has all the attention he could want.

This method can be used in many different scenarios, and you will find that it works wonders. Instead of the dog 'training you' to do what he wants, you have turned the tables, and your dog will have renewed respect for you.

Interrupting behaviour

There are times when you want to call an immediate halt to your dog's behaviour. He may have just jumped on the sofa, or you may have caught him reaching up to steal some food from a kitchen surface. He has already committed the 'crime', so your aim is to stop him – to interrupt his behaviour – and then to redirect his attention.

As we have seen, you can do this verbally, but in a more extreme situation, when you know that a simple "No" will not work, you can try something a little more dramatic. If you get a can and fill it with pebbles, it will make a really loud noise when you shake it or throw it. The same effect can be achieved with purpose-made training discs. The dog will be startled and stop what he is doing. Even better, the dog will not associate the unpleasant noise with you. He will turn and look at you, wondering what has happened, and this gives you the perfect opportunity to call the dog to you and give him lots of praise. You are not praising him for his 'bad' behaviour. You have stopped him in his tracks, and now you are starting afresh and praising him for coming to you.

Good manners

You need to teach your dog basic training exercises (see page 106), but alongside this you want to establish good manners at home.

Mouthing

It is natural for puppies to mouth and nip, but it is important to put a stop to this behaviour at an early stage, particularly if you have young children in the family.

- Show your puppy you have a treat, and then close your fist on it. The puppy will try to get the treat – jumping up at you, scrabbling with his paws, and then mouthing your hand.

- If necessary, growl at your puppy, or say "No" in a firm low-pitched voice, but do not attempt to restrain your puppy or to move your hand out of his way. This will only encourage him to renew his efforts.

- If you do not react, the puppy will soon realise he is not getting what he wants, so he will pause to consider his next move. At this moment, open your hand and give him the treat.

- Keep practising, and the puppy will learn that when he 'mugs you' he gets nothing, and when he is quiet and still, he is given the treat.

- As you give the treat, introduce the verbal cue, "Gently" and if your pup attempts to snatch, close your fist and then try again. The puppy is learning to curb his natural behaviour, and to learn the 'right' behaviour when he is dealing with people.

Giving up toys on request

As part of his early education, a puppy needs to understand that although he is allowed to play with the toys you provide – you remain in charge. You 'own' his toys and he must give them up on request.

The reason for this is that some dogs have a tendency to 'guard' treasured possessions, and this behaviour could escalate into growling – or even biting – if someone tries to take the 'prize' away.

- Place some treats near at hand, but out of your puppy's reach. Then have a game with your puppy, using a tuggy type toy, where you can be interactive.

- When you decide the game is over, relax your hand, but do not let go of the toy. When a toy is no longer 'alive' it loses much of its interest for a puppy.

- Your pup may leave go of the toy or he may hold on, but because it is still, he will loosen his grip. Now offer a treat in exchange for the toy. Do this calmly and quietly – do not snatch the toy away, or it will 'come to life' and be exciting again.

- Keep practising, and when your puppy understands what you want, introduce the verbal cue "Give".

Good
manners at
meal times

Food is a top priority for dogs and meal times are a high spot of the day. It is important that your puppy learns good manners around his food bowl, or he may become demanding when you are preparing it, or possessive when you have put his bowl down.

- When you are preparing your puppy's food, he should remain quiet and not attempt to jump up.

- If he barks or attempts to jump up to reach the food, suspend all preparations, and only recommence when your puppy is calm and quiet.

- When the food is ready, ask your puppy to "Sit", and wait a couple of seconds before putting the bowl down. Your pup is learning that you are in charge of his food, and he must co-operate with you in order to get it.

- Try dropping a few extra treats in the bowl while your puppy is eating. This teaches him to welcome your 'interference' and will curb any tendency he has to guard his food bowl.

What is clicker training?

What is clicker training?

This is a system of training that is easy to use, and very effective, as the dog knows exactly when he has got something right, which can avoid a great deal of confusion and misunderstanding.

A clicker is a small matchbox-shaped training aid, with a metal tongue that makes a click when it is pressed. All you have to do is to teach your dog that when he hears a click, a reward will follow. You can then use the clicker to mark correct behaviour, signalling to the dog he has done what you want, and, by association, he knows a reward will follow.

Introducing a clicker

- Prepare some treats and go to an area that is free from distractions. Allow your dog to wander and when he stops to look at you, click and reward by throwing him a treat. This means he will not crowd you, but will go looking for the treat. Repeat a couple of times. If your dog is very easily distracted, you may need to start this exercise with the dog on a lead.

- After a few clicks, your dog will understand that if he hears a click, he will get a treat. He must now learn that he must 'earn' a click. This time, when your dog looks at you, wait a little longer before clicking and then reward him.

- When your dog is working for a click and giving you his attention, you can introduce a cue or command word, such as "Watch". Repeat a few times, using the cue. You now have a dog that understands the clicker and will give you his attention when you ask him to "Watch".

Tips for clicker training

Get your timing right, so you click at the precise moment your dog is responding correctly.

Prepare bite-size treats, so training is not held up every time your dog gets a treat.

Do not use multiple clicks to 'gee up' your dog, or use the clicker as a way of getting his attention. A single click, which means: "Ok, this is what I want", is all you need.

When you are training a new exercise, click and reward your dog for every stage. When he understands the exercise, click at the end of the exercise. As a dog becomes more experienced, you can string a number of exercises together, and your dog will keep on working, knowing a click – and a reward – will come at the end of the sequence.

If your dog is finding an exercise difficult, go back to basics. Click and reward for every stage, so that he understands exactly what you want.

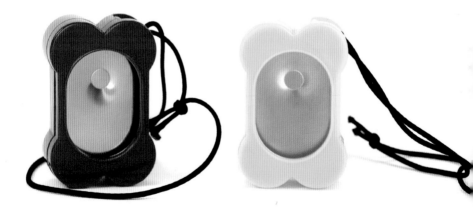

Basic training
exercises

Basic training exercises

Clicker training is used in the exercises outlined below. This is not essential, but if you are not using a clicker, make sure you reward your dog at frequent intervals so he understands what you want.

Sit

This is easy to teach, and most dogs pick it up in no time.

- Show your dog you have a treat in your hand, and hold it just above his head.

- As he looks up at the treat, he will naturally go back on his hindquarters and sit. Click and reward.

- Practice a few times so your dog knows what you want, and then add the verbal cue, "Sit".

If your dog has a favourite toy, you can use this as a lure, and reward him with a game. This applies to all training exercises.

Down

You can start with your dog in a sit or when he is standing.

- Hold a treat just in front of your dog's nose and lower it slowly towards the ground.

- Your dog may try to paw at your hand to get the treat, but close your fist, and wait for your dog to try another strategy.

- His next attempt to get the treat will be to lower his forequarters – wait a few seconds, and his hindquarters will follow. Click and reward as soon as he is in the down position.

- If your dog is reluctant, stroke him along his back to encourage him to go down.

- Keep practising and, when your dog understands what you want, you can use the verbal cue, "Down".

In time you can withdraw the lure and use a hand signal. With practice, your dog will respond to the verbal cue alone.

Stand

This is not an essential exercise, but it very useful if you want to groom your dog or if he needs to be examined by a vet.

- Start with your dog in the sit, and show him you have a treat.

- Draw your hand away from the dog's nose in a straight line, and he will move up and towards you to reach it. Click and reward.

- If your dog is going straight back into the sit, put your hand on his underside, and gently stroke him to encourage him to stay in the stand.

- When your dog understands what you want, introduce the verbal cue, "Stand".

Wait

This can be used when you want your dog to stay still for a few moments until you give the next cue. For example, when you open the car door and you want your dog to "Wait" until you have attached his lead.

- Attach a lead, and ask your dog to "Sit".

- Stand at his side and take one step away with your back facing the dog. Hold your arm downwards, with the palm towards the dog's face. This hand signal is effectively 'blocking' him, so he knows he should not move.

- Step back to stand alongside your dog. Click and reward.

- Keep practicing, going to the end of your dog's lead. Click and reward every time. You can now introduce the verbal cue, "Wait".

- Gradually increase the amount of time you can leave your dog before returning to his side. When he is rock steady, try him off lead. In time, he will respond to the verbal cue and will no longer need the hand signal.

Stay

This exercise is used when you want your dog to "Stay" in position for some time. He needs to relax rather than be on the alert, anticipating the next cue.

- A dog can be taught to "Stay" in the sit, stand or down positions. However, it is best to start with the down, as your dog will be more comfortable and this will encourage him to stay in position.

- To differentiate this exercise from the wait, face your dog and take one step back, using the same hand signal. Return to stand in front of him, and then click and reward.

- Keep practicing, gradually building up the time and distance you can leave him.

- Introduce the verbal cue, "Stay" and your dog will understand that this is a different exercise from the "Wait".

In advanced Obedience competitions, dogs have to stay in position for 10 minutes with their owners out of sight – so this may be something to aspire to!

Lead training

Going out for a walk is one of the
pleasures of dog ownership, but not if
your dog lags behind, sniffing at every
lamp-post, or worse still, charges ahead
and pulls your shoulder out of joint!

Establishing good lead work is not difficult, but it
does demand some time and effort. Regardless of
the type of dog you own, it is best to start early on
before your dog has got into bad habits. If you have
a large breed, it is essential, or you will find yourself
involved in a test of strength.

The aim of this exercise is to train your dog to walk
on a loose lead, focusing his attention on you when
required.

- To begin with, attach a lead and allow your puppy
  to wander at will, making sure the lead does not
  become caught on anything.

- Next pick up the lead, and follow your puppy so he
  gets used to you holding the lead.

- Now encourage the puppy to walk alongside you. The easiest way to do this is to show him you have treats; when he is in the correct position, click and reward.

- Build on this, gradually extending the intervals between giving treats so your puppy is maintaining the correct position for longer. You can now introduce a verbal cue such as "Heel" or "Close".

- If your puppy attempts to lag behind or pull ahead, come to a complete standstill. This will teach him that if he is not in the correct position, everything grinds to a halt. Re-focus his attention on you, and then set off again.

Coming
when called

Your dog will consider free running
exercise one of his greatest treats,
but you can only allow this if you have
access to a safe exercise area – and you
can rely on your dog to come back to
you when he is called.

The mistake most people make is to be over-
protective with a puppy and not allow him off lead
– and then they are surprised when their 'teenager'
goes wild at his first taste of freedom.

• A puppy will instinctively follow you, so capitalise
  on this from day one. Call your puppy from across
  the room, or from one room to another. When he
  responds, make a big fuss of him – give him a
  treat or have a game – so he learns it is always
  rewarding to come to you.

- Venture out into the garden, and try calling your puppy when he is busy investigating. Make a really big fuss of him as he has left something he wanted to do to come to you.

- If your puppy is slow to respond, you are not being exciting enough. Use a higher tone of voice, wave your arms about, run off in the opposite direction – it does not matter how silly you look or feel, your puppy must see you as the most fun person in the world.

- When your puppy responds – even though he may have taken his time – make sure you still make a huge fuss of him and reward him with treats or a game. A puppy must never be told off for a slow response, or he will not bother coming back next time.

Finally...

Training a dog is hard work and it can require patience, but it should never be looked on as a chore. The time you spend training your dog is very special; it gives you the opportunity to relate to each other and to build up a close bond. It is also very rewarding, regardless of whether you are working with a family pet or the next Obedience Champion. But most of all it is lots of fun – and the greatest reward of all is owning an outstanding companion that you can be truly proud of.

Weights & measures

If you prefer your units in pounds and inches, you can use this conversion chart:

Length in inches	Length in cm	Weight in kg	Weight in lbs
1	2.5	0.5	1.1
2	5.1	0.7	1.5
3	7.6	1	2.2
4	10.2	1.5	3.3
5	12.7	2	4.4
8	20.3	3	6.6
10	25.4	4	8.8
15	38.1	5	11

Measurements rounded to 1 decimal place.